Islam:

Signs, Symbols, and Stories

Cath Senker

press™

New York

Published in 2010 by The Rosen Publishing Group Inc.
29 East 21st Street, New York, NY 10010

Copyright © 2010 Wayland/
The Rosen Publishing Group, Inc.

First Edition

Library of Congress Cataloging-in-Publication Data

Senker, Cath.
  Islam:signs, symbols, stories / Cath Senker.
      p. cm. -- (Religious signs, symbols, and stories)
  Includes index.
  ISBN 978-1-4358-3040-0 (library binding)
  ISBN 978-1-4358-3048-6 (paperback)
  ISBN 978-1-4358-3056-1 (6-pack)
  1. Islam--Juvenile literature. I. Title.
  BP161.3.S46 2010
  297--dc22
                              2008051915

Manufactured in China

Disclaimer
Although every effort has been made to offer accurate and clearly expressed information, the author and publisher acknowledge
that some explanations may not be relevant to those who practice their faith in a different way.

Acknowledgements
The author and publisher would like to thank the following for allowing their pictures to be reproduced in this publication:
Cover illustrations: Emmanuel Cerisier (both); ArkReligion.com/Alamy: 13, 18; Chris Fairclough: cover (inset), 8, 10, 12, 14,
15 (both), 16, 19, 20, 21; Fred de Noyelle/Godong/Corbis: 6; JTB Photo Communications/ Alamy: 29; Robert
O'Dea/Arcaid/Corbis: 4; Sally & Richard Greenhill/Alamy: 26, 28; Studio DL/Corbis: 23.

The author would like to thank the following for permission to reproduce material in this book: p.11 'The Beggar by the Masjid'
by Shaikh Sa'eed ibn Musfir from Islam is for you (www.islamisforyou.com); p.13 'This is the way we make Wudu' by Asma
Mohyudeen from Mutma'inaa (www.geocities.com); p.15 translation of Al-Fatiha from (www.angelfire.com); p.17 activity
based on Karen's Prayer Beads (www.angelfire.com); p.21 'For Allah' by S. E. (Safiyyah) Jihad Levine from Islamic Poetry
(www.islamicpoetry.org); p.23 Translation of Qur'an story drawn from IslamiCity (http://www.islamicity.com; p.25 recipe
drawn from all recipes (www.allrecipes.com); p.27 recipe drawn from Festivals of India:(www.festivals inindia.net).
With special thanks to Zohal Azizi.

The author and publisher would like to thank the following models: Celine Clark, Isobel Grace, Hari Johal, and Charlie Pengelly.

With special thanks to Dr. S. K. Haque and Huma Ashraf.

**Note to parents and teachers: The projects in this book are designed to be made by children. However, we do
recommend adult supervision at all times since the Publisher cannot be held responsible for any injury caused while
undertaking any activities.**

Contents

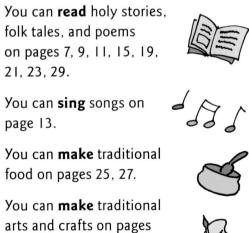

Activities

There are lots of activities throughout this book.

You can **read** holy stories, folk tales, and poems on pages 7, 9, 11, 15, 19, 21, 23, 29.

You can **sing** songs on page 13.

You can **make** traditional food on pages 25, 27.

You can **make** traditional arts and crafts on pages 5, 17.

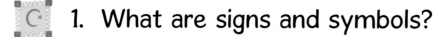

Signs and symbols

A sign usually has one clear meaning. A street sign that says "stop" means "stop" and nothing else.

A symbol can have different meanings. All religions use symbols. The color green is a symbol for Muslims. It stands for nature and the earth. There is usually green on the flags of Muslim countries.

Muslims have symbols, but they do not use any pictures to show their **prophets**. This is because they don't know what the prophets looked like. Also, they believe that pictures stop people from focusing on God.

*Islamic designs often include the name **Allah** and other words from the **Qur'an** (Koran) in Arabic.*

Islamic patterns

Although they do not use images, Muslims use beautiful patterns with different shapes to decorate their buildings.

See if you can copy these Islamic patterns. Then see if you can make up your own, similar ones.

You will need:

Some paper or card
Pens and pencils
You can use glitter or paint

The Qiblah and the crescent moon and star

The most important sign for Muslims is the **Qiblah**. It is usually an arrow pointing in the direction of the **Ka'ba** in **Mecca** (Makkah), where Islam began. All over the world, Muslims pray facing the Ka'ba.

The crescent moon and star are often seen together as a symbol of Islam. The five-pointed star stands for the **Five Pillars of Islam**, which every Muslim should carry out. They are:

1. Shahadah—belief in one God
2. Salah—prayer
3. Zakah—charity
4. Sawm—**fasting** at **Ramadan**
5. Hajj—**pilgrimage** to Mecca in Saudi Arabia.

A Qiblah sign on the wall in a Muslim country, shows the direction of Mecca, so that Muslims know which way to face for prayer.

Saving the Moon

Mullah Nasruddin is a popular funny character in stories in the Middle East and Central Asia. Some stories are just amusing, but others teach a lesson.

Mullah Nasruddin was walking past a well one night during Ramadan. He peered into the water below and was shocked to see the moon down there. "I must save the moon!" he thought. "Otherwise there will be no new moon, and the month of Ramadan will never end." He threw a rope into the well, and it got caught on a rock. Nasruddin pulled hard on the rope. Suddenly, it gave way, and he was thrown backward. Lying on the ground, he noticed the moon up in the sky. "Lucky I came along to help you out!" he cried happily.

Outside the mosque

Muslims worship at a **mosque**. Some mosques are specially built with a large dome. The perfect shape of the dome shows that Allah is perfect and everlasting. It is humans who make mistakes!

A tall tower called a **minaret** stretches toward the sky from the side of the mosque. In the early days of Islam, Muslims were called to prayer from the highest rooftop near the mosque. Then people started to build mosques with towers especially for making the call to prayer. The call to prayer is still made from the minaret today.

This mosque was built from an old church. You can see the minaret on the left.

Let's read the Qur'an

The Prophet's Night Journey

One night, the Prophet Muhammad ﷺ had an extraordinary experience. He was taken from his home in Mecca to Jerusalem. From a rock there, he rose up to the sky.

As he moved through the seven heavens, Muhammad ﷺ met all the great prophets of the past, including Moses ﷺ and Jesus ﷺ, and asked their advice. Finally, he reached Allah. Allah spoke to Muhammad ﷺ. He told him that Muslims should pray five times a day.

More than 50 years after the Prophet's ﷺ death, the Muslim ruler, Caliph Abd al-Malik, built the Dome of the Rock over the rock from which Muhammad ﷺ had risen to heaven. It was the first great mosque to be built.

Note: When Muslims say the name of one of the prophets, they always say "Peace Be Upon Him" afterward as a sign of respect. In this book, this is shown as ﷺ.

Inside the mosque

Inside the mosque are signs, symbols, and objects used in worship. In the wall, there is a niche (small, hollow place) called the **mihrab**. It shows the Qiblah sign, the direction of Mecca.

People perform prayers together at the mosque.

Muslims come to the mosque to express their faith in Allah and perform prayers together. They put money in the collection box to help the running of the mosque. Muslims also give money to charity (although not always in the mosque itself). It is a vital symbol of the Islamic faith to help others.

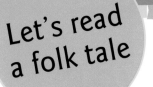

The Beggar by the Mosque

A rich man was walking back to his stylish, gleaming car near the Great Mosque in Mecca. A poor man begging on the street asked him for money, "Please, for the sake of Allah!" he cried. The rich man did not want to help. "Allah will provide," he replied. "Don't worry, I know that," said the beggar. The two stared at each other for a moment, and the rich man drove away.

A cloth seller sitting nearby had watched the scene. Although she was poor herself, she gave the beggar some money, and he went on his way.

Meanwhile, the rich man was feeling guilty. He returned to the mosque with a big note in his hand to give to the beggar—but he could not find him. Instead, he gave it to the woman who was selling cloth. The story goes to show that if you give, you, too, will receive.

Preparing for prayer

Muslims believe it is important to be clean and pure for worship. They perform special actions as symbols of purity, both at the mosque and when they perform prayers at home.

People take their shoes off before entering the prayer hall. It is to keep the mosque clean and show respect for the place of worship.

People take their shoes off before going into the prayer hall in the mosque.

Worshipers perform **wudu—ritual** washing. They wash their hands, arms, mouth, nose, face, neck, and feet. Wudu is a symbol for cleansing the five senses: sight, taste, smell, hearing, and touch.

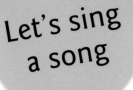

Let's sing a song

This is the way we make wudu

This song is sung to the tune of "Here we go round the mulberry bush."

*This is the way we wash our hands,
Wash our hands, wash our hands,
This is the way we wash our hands,
When we make wudu.*

Following verses:

*Rinse our mouth
Clean our nose
Wash our face
Clean our arms
Wipe our head
Clean our ears
Wipe our neck
Wash our feet*

By Asma Mohyudeen

Symbols of prayer

Muslims pray five times a day, between dawn and nighttime. Prayer time is symbolic. It means setting aside normal life for a short while to focus on Allah. There are winter and summer prayer times.

Muslims pray using special words and movements. The movements are called **rak'ahs** (see opposite). For example, *ruku* is bending forward with a straight back and placing your hands on your knees. It shows that you respect and love Allah. *Sujud* is kneeling down and touching the ground with your forehead, nose, hands, knees, and toes. It shows that you love Allah more than yourself.

The prayer times change depending on the time of year. Clocks in the mosque show the prayer times.

The Fatiha

The Fatiha is the first verse of the Qur'an (Koran). It is said at the start of each rak'ah.

All praise is for Allah, the Lord of the Universe, the most Merciful [ready to forgive people], the most Kind.

Master of the Day of Judgement [the day when Allah will judge whether people have lived a good or a bad life].

You alone we worship, from You alone we seek help.

Guide us along the straight path—the path of those whom You favored, not of those who earned Your anger or went astray [the wrong way].

Prayer beads

Muslims sometimes use **subhah beads** (also called tasbih beads). The word *subhah* comes from the Arabic word "to praise." There are either 33 or 99 beads. The 99 beads stand for the 99 names of Allah in the Qur'an. Worshipers thumb through the beads and count the 99 names. It helps them to think about Allah.

Subhah beads are usually made from wood. Large beads are used as markers after the 33rd and 66th bead to help worshipers keep count. The largest bead stands for the name Allah, and it completes the subhah.

Subhah beads are used in prayer.

Subhah beads

You will need:

About 100 plastic or wooden beads

Two larger beads and one even larger to stand for the name Allah

Stiff cord or rope from a craft store or a long shoelace

1. Tie a knot at one end of the cord. Thread the largest bead.

2. Thread 33 small beads and then one of the larger beads.

3. Repeat step 2.

4. Thread another 33 beads.

5. Poke the end of the cord back through the largest bead. Knot the two ends of the cord. Cut off any extra cord.

The holy book

The Qur'an (Koran) is the holy book of Islam. According to Muslims, it is formed of Allah's words, given to the people through the Prophet Muhammad ﷺ. It is written in beautiful Arabic poetry.

The Qur'an is a guide. It shows Muslims how to behave toward each other and how to respect Allah and the world he created.

As a symbol of its importance, worshipers treat the Qur'an with great care. They often place it on a special stool called a **kursi**. To Muslims, **blessings** flow from the sound of the words in the Qur'an. They learn to recite it in Arabic, verse by verse. Words from the Qur'an are often used in **calligraphy**. They are a symbol of Allah.

Words from the Qur'an are often used on Muslim buildings. The Arabic words on this mosque say "There is no God but Allah."

Let's read the Qur'an

Kindness

The Qur'an guides people. This verse shows that being kind to others is central to the Muslim faith.

107.001 Hast thou observed him who belieth religion?

[Have you seen the man who does not follow his religion properly?]

107.002 That is he who repelleth the orphan,

[He doesn't help the orphans.]

107.003 And urgeth not the feeding of the needy.

[He doesn't worry about feeding needy people.]

107.004 Ah, woe unto worshipers

107.005 Who are heedless of their prayer;

[There will be trouble for worshipers who do not pay attention to their prayers—]

107.006 Who would be seen (at worship)

[the people who are seen at worship]

107.007 Yet refuse small kindnesses!

[but do not help others at all.]

The hijab and clothing for prayer

The Qur'an teaches that people should dress **modestly** and not wear short or tight clothes. Some Muslim girls and women cover their head with a scarf called a **hijab**. Dressing modestly is a symbol of respect for themselves and for Allah.

Muslims often wear special clothing for prayer. Both men and women cover their head. Men might put on a white robe and prayer cap. Some women may wear a black **burka** or other clothing that covers the body and limbs.

This family has dressed for prayers and study at the mosque.

For Allah

I wear my hijab for Allah,
Not for my father
Not for my husband
Not for my brother
Not for any other

Than Allah

I cover myself for Allah,
No one makes me
No one forsakes me [stops me]
No one rejects me
No one subjects me

But Allah

My modesty is for Allah,
Commanded in Qu'ran
For Him and no one else
Seeking His reward

Moving closer toward Allah.

by S. E. (Safiyyah) Jihad
Levine, U.S.A.

Welcoming a new baby

When a baby is born, prayers are whispered into its ears. In this way, the baby starts life as a Muslim. A small piece of date or honey is rubbed into its gums. This is to make the baby sweet and well behaved.

The naming ceremony takes place a week later. The baby's head is shaved as a symbol of a new life. The family gives the weight of the hair in gold or silver to the poor.

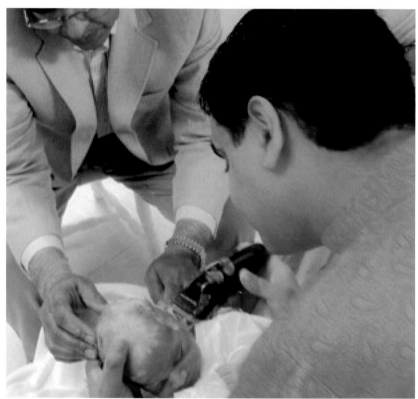

Shaving the head is a symbol that the baby will serve God.

Around the same time, a baby boy is **circumcised**. It is a sign of belonging to the Islamic faith.

Love your mother

Islam teaches children to
be kind to their parents,
especially their mothers.
Mothers have a special
place in Islam.

*A man once asked the
Prophet ﷺ, "Who should
I **honor** most?" Muhammad ﷺ answered, "Your mother." Then
the man asked, "Who should I honor next?" Muhammad ﷺ
said, "Your mother." The man continued: "Who should I honor
after that?" The Prophet ﷺ replied, "Your mother." The man
asked once more, "But who should I honor after my mother?"
"Your father," responded Muhammad ﷺ.*

(Bukhari and Muslim)

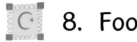

Ramadan

During the Islamic month of Ramadan, Muslim adults do not eat or drink between dawn and sunset. They break their fast at sunset with dates and water, and eat a good meal. Then they wake up very early to have breakfast before dawn.

Fasting is a symbol of self-control and learning not to be greedy. It also reminds Muslims what it's like to be poor and go hungry. The aim of fasting is to focus on prayer and good deeds.

During Ramadan, families gather after sunset to eat together.

Rice pudding with dates

Ask an adult to help you cook

Here is a simple meal for suhor, the meal eaten just before dawn during Ramadan.

You will need:

2 cups cooked white rice
2 cups milk
3 tablespoons white sugar
15 dates, pitted and chopped

1. *Blend the rice until it forms a rough mixture.*

2. *Put the rice in a pan and stir in the milk, sugar, and dates.*

3. *Cook on low heat for about 20 minutes, stirring regularly.*

4. *When the dates are soft, your pudding is ready.*

Id ul-Fitr

After a month going without food and beverages during the day, it is time to celebrate. **Id ul-Fitr** is an important festival at the end of Ramadan. Muslims put on new clothes and enjoy a special dinner.

Islam stands for a caring society. The rich help the poor. As a symbol of their ideals, richer people give money to charity at Id. Then poorer people can enjoy the festival, too. Nobody is left out of the celebrations.

At Id ul-Fitr, people enjoy delicious food with family and friends.

Recipe for seviyan

Ask an adult to help you cook

This Id ul-Fitr recipe is from India. You can leave out the nuts if you are allergic to them.

You will need:

2 oz (50 g) vermicelli noodles or rice noodles

2 tablespoons raisins

2 tablespoons nuts

2 cardamom pods, powdered

half can sweetened condensed milk

1 pint ($1/2$ liter) whole milk

1 tablespoon butter

1. *Heat the butter in a pan and fry the vermicelli until it is light brown.*

2. *Boil the milk.*

3. *Add the condensed milk, vermicelli, and cardamom powder to the milk.*

4. *Cook for 2 to 3 minutes, until the vermicelli is soft.*

5. *Put the raisins and nuts on the top.*

Id ul-Adha

At **Id ul-Adha**, Muslims remember how Allah tested the Prophet Ibrahim's ﷺ faith. At this festival, families have a sheep, goat, or cow **slaughtered**. The **sacrifice** is a symbol that Muslims should be willing to give up their wants or needs for Allah. They should be prepared to make sacrifices in their own lives. Muslims must perform their duty to Allah, even when it is hard to do so.

As a symbol of kindness, families share the meat with friends, neighbors, and poor people.

Id ul-Adha is a time for sharing. The boy offers a dish of home-cooked food to his neighbors.

Ibrahim's ﷺ sacrifice

This story comes from the Qur'an. It is in the Jewish and Christian holy books, too.

Ibrahim ﷺ was a wealthy man who lived with his two wives, Hajar and Sarah. With Hajar, he had a son called Isma'il ﷺ.

Ibrahim ﷺ was humble and devoted to Allah. One day, Allah decided to put Ibrahim's ﷺ faith to the test. He ordered him to sacrifice his only son. Ibrahim ﷺ was shocked, but he believed completely in Allah and accepted his command.

With a heavy heart, Ibrahim ﷺ took his son to Mina, the place of sacrifice near Mecca. He got ready to perform the sacrifice, and brave Isma'il ﷺ prepared to die. At the last moment, Allah provided a ram in Isma'il's ﷺ place, and the boy was saved.

As part of their pilgrimage to Mecca, Muslims visit Mina to remember these events.

Allah God.

blessings Allah's help and protection.

burka A long, loose garment that covers the entire body.

calligraphy Decorative writing.

circumcised To cut off the foreskin from the penis.

fasting To go without food and water for religious reasons.

Five Pillars of Islam The five duties of every Muslim: belief in one God; prayer; giving to charity; fasting at Ramadan; and making a pilgrimage to Mecca.

hijab A scarf that some Muslim girls and women wear to cover their hair.

honor Offer great respect to someone.

Id ul-Adha The festival to celebrate how Ibrahim passed the test of his faith in Allah.

Id ul-Fitr The festival to celebrate the end of Ramadan.

Ka'ba The shrine to Allah in Mecca.

kursi The stand for the Qur'an.

Mecca (Makkah) The city in modern Saudi Arabia where the Prophet Muhammad was born and where he started to teach the message of Islam.

mihrab The small, hollow place in the mosque wall that shows the direction of Mecca.

minaret The tower from which the call to prayer is given.

modestly Dressing so you don't show off your body.

mosque The place where Muslims meet, pray, and study.

pilgrimage A journey to a holy place for religious reasons.

prophets People sent by Allah to teach the people and bring them his messages.

Qiblah The direction of Mecca, usually shown with an arrow.

Qur'an (Koran) The Muslims' holy book. According to Muslims, it contains the words of Allah, as given to the Prophet Muhammad .

rak'ahs A series of movements in prayer.

Ramadan The Muslim month during which Muslims do not eat or drink between sunrise and sunset.

ritual An action that is always done in the same way, as part of a religious ceremony.

sacrifice To kill something to offer to Allah. It also means to give up something important in your own life for the sake of something even more important.

slaughtered The killing of an animal for its meat.

wudu Ritual washing in order to be pure and clean for prayer.

Books to read

Islam for Children
by Ahmad von Denffer (Islamic Foundation, 2007)

Islamic Stories (Traditional Religious Tales)
by Anita Ganeri (Picture Window Books, 2006)

Muslim Child: Understanding Islam Through Stories and Poems
by Rukhsana Khan (Albert Whitman and Company, 2002)

Ramadan: Islamic Holy Month
by Terri Sievert (First Facts Books, 2006)

What You Will See Inside a Mosque
by Aisha Karen Kahn (Skylight Paths Publishing, 2003)

Web Sites

Due to the changing nature of Internet links, PowerKids Press has developed an online list of Web sites related to the subject of this book. This site is updated regularly. Please use this link to access this list: www.powerkidslinks.com/sss/islam